CARD GAMES FOR ONE OR TWO

CARD GAMES

GAMES

FOR

ONE OR TWO

52 GAMES TO KNOW AND PLAY

DUSTIN RAMSDELL

ROCKRIDGE
PRESS

For general information on our other products and services or to obtain technical support, please contact our Customer Care Department within the United States at (866) 744-2665, or outside the United States at (510) 253-0500.

Rockridge Press publishes its books in a variety of electronic and print formats. Some content that appears in print may not be available in electronic books, and vice versa.

Interior and Cover Designer: Angela Navarra
Art Producer: Megan Baggott
Editor: Van Van Cleave
Production Manager: Jose Olivera

Author photo courtesy of Marianna McGinley.

Paperback ISBN: 978-1-63878-374-9
eBook ISBN: 978-1-63878-770-9
R0

CONTENTS

INTRODUCTION

consider myself a lifelong gamer. For as long as I can remember, I've played board games, video games, and card games. I enjoy each type of game for different reasons, and they have all come in and out of my life at various stages. I've had phases when I've focused more on one game or another. For example, sometimes I don't play video games because they rely on expensive hardware. Other times, I may not have enough people around to play a board game. Card games, however, are in a category all their own. A good card game is always available as long as you have a simple deck. To me, the reliability and simplicity of cards is part of their charm.

Memories of playing card games span my entire life. I can fondly recall playing intense games of War with my older brother. I also played Solitaire to pass the time when I was younger. Card games were also always there for my family whenever the power went out and we needed something to do by candlelight. Even now, I look forward to sharing various card games with my daughter as she grows up. They're truly timeless games that span generations and give us a great opportunity to show friends and family something new and have a lot of fun in the process. I'm sure many people have cherished memories that revolve around card games.

Many card games date back hundreds of years and have storied pasts in countries all over the world. They've always allowed people to come together, and even now, they serve as a valuable way to help us disconnect from technology and be more present with others in our lives. Card games are simple, portable, accessible, and easy to play. While the world has changed, card games have remained a constant source of entertainment.

Card games are more than just a fun pastime. They can also be a great way to build new skills and ways of thinking. You can learn about patience, memory, concentration, strategy, and math by playing cards. Although often simple in concept, card games often require skill-building and practice to master them. With such an abundant variety of games, there is no limit to the new skills and experiences you can gain.

This book will show you how to play an array of great card games on your own or with one other person. These games can serve as icebreakers, team-builders, date activities, or family night features, as well as simply a way for you to be more present in a world filled with noise and distractions. I hope that after you read this book, you will feel inspired to play some newly discovered card games or return to some of your old favorites. Keep this book on hand and refer to it while you're learning any new games.

I hope you enjoy learning about these games as much as I enjoyed writing about them. Let's dive in!

GETTING STARTED WITH ONE- AND TWO-PLAYER GAMES

As we begin our journey exploring one- and two-player games, we need to review the essentials of card games and the language surrounding them. This will make the reading experience easier for you since you'll have some familiarity with the lingo being used. You'll also learn how to play card games well and how to avoid common pitfalls. Knowing the ins and outs will also help you teach others how to play with you when the time comes. With that in mind, let's get into these essentials.

CARD GAME BASICS

Let's start at the beginning with the foundations of all card games. In this section, I'll define what a deck is and what to know to make sure you're prepared. I'll also walk you through how to shuffle and deal cards so that you can start your games on the right foot. Although this information may feel unnecessary to some readers, we often take for granted what we know about something as common as playing cards. The last time you learned the basics could have been many years ago, so whether you're learning for the first time or brushing up on what you already know, there's something here for everyone.

THE DECK

For any card game, you'll obviously need a deck of cards. All the games included in this book use standard 52-card decks, which may also be referred to as French or Anglo-American decks of cards.

One deck of cards consists of four suits: Hearts, Diamonds, Spades, and Clubs. Within each of these suits, there are 13 cards: Ace (or A), 2, 3, 4, 5, 6, 7, 8, 9, 10, Jack, Queen, and King. The Jack, Queen, and King cards will often look quite different for each suit, and the text and the symbols on most cards are often colored red or black within the same deck. Some games may require you to play by color. For these, please note that Hearts and Diamonds are considered red, and Spades and Clubs are considered black. Nowadays, there are so many different brands of card decks that the look of the cards may vary quite a bit. As you learn new card games, you may find it helpful to stick with a classic deck versus a more artistic one or one that's based on your favorite television show.

Most standard decks also include Joker cards, but most games don't use them. I recommend you keep them with your deck, but usually you can set them aside immediately before shuffling. Also, some games will require multiple decks to play. It can be beneficial to have several decks on hand, just in case. You can also ask the person you're playing with to bring their own deck.

DEALING

Once you're ready to start playing, you'll need to shuffle your cards. Now, shuffling can feel like an intimidating skill to learn when you watch someone who is really experienced, but there are a lot of resources for tips on how to shuffle cards better. The basic principle here is to make sure each individual card is moving throughout the deck. There are various strategies to do this, some requiring more dexterity than others, but even simply splitting a deck repeatedly can help. Taking the time to practice will eventually give you the skills to ensure the deck is quickly and thoroughly shuffled. A poorly shuffled deck can hinder most games, especially if you're breaking open a new deck.

Once you've shuffled the deck, you're ready to deal the appropriate cards to all the players, whether it's just you or you and a partner. Depending on the game, each person's hand could be just a few cards or half of the entire deck. Also of note, the dealer can sometimes play an important role in kicking off the flow of the game in addition to dealing out the cards. The dealer may need to play first or make some sort of decision to get the game going. When the dealer has a responsibility, it will be noted in the game directions.

Finally, for some games, like Solitaire, you'll need to set up the cards properly before playing. When setup is necessary, it will be mentioned in the game notes and illustrated.

• • CARD GAME TRIVIA • •

Here are some fun facts to think about while you're practicing your shuffling!

1. In Las Vegas casinos, card decks are replaced every 12 hours on average, depending on how often they're used.

2. The United States Playing Card Company, known for their classic Bicycle Playing Cards, makes more than 100 million card decks every year.

3. There are several wild connections between a standard card deck and the calendar year. For example, there are four suits equal to the four seasons of the year, 13 values equal to the 13 weeks in a quarter, and 52 cards equal to the 52 weeks in the year.

4. During World War II, special decks of playing cards were shared with American soldiers who were being held as German prisoners. These cards revealed maps when they got wet, helping lead some of the men to freedom.

5. According to Guinness World Records, the current record for the fastest time to deal a deck of playing cards is held by an Indian man, Arpit Lall, who was able to do it in 16.92 seconds.

TYPES OF CARD GAMES

There are dozens of popular card games that we'll be covering in this book. For ease, I've organized them into six categories based on the main goal of the game. To this end, the categories are Patience Games, Capturing Games, Shedding Games, Matching Games, Trick-Taking Games, and Vying Games. These groups provide an easy way to contextualize what types of games are out there and will also help you navigate the book when looking for a game you want to play. It's worth noting that there is some overlap between these groups, but the categories are generally agreed upon by card aficionados. In this section, I'll give a brief description of the categories and provide examples of games that fit into each one.

PATIENCE GAMES

Patience games are single-player experiences in which the player is typically trying to manipulate cards to arrange them by their suit. These games are often discussed as being on a spectrum of "open" to "closed," in which "open" means that all cards are revealed to the player and "closed" means no cards are revealed. There can also be "half-open" games, in which cards become revealed to the player over time. Each kind of patience game produces a different experience and uses different skills. Any of the variations of Solitaire (Classic, Spider, Wish) are classified as patience games. Some cardplayers around the world even call classic Solitaire "Patience."

CAPTURING GAMES

Capturing games involve trying to obtain certain cards, a certain number of cards, or simply as many cards as possible. There may be point values attributed to certain cards in the deck, which would change how the game is played. The premise of these games is simple, but they can easily be altered into fun variations. They are also easy to learn, making them ideal for a game night with children. Some examples include Go Fish and Slapjack.

SHEDDING GAMES

Shedding games are the opposite of capturing games. The goal here is to be the first to get rid of all your cards or at least to avoid being the last one left with a card. They tend to be quick to play and add a competitive aspect without requiring too much skill. Shedding games are also accessible and fun for younger players. Some examples of games in this category are Old Maid or Crazy Eights. The popular card game Uno also falls into this category.

MATCHING GAMES

Famous for their simplicity and clear objective, matching games are another popular category of card games. The goal for games in this category is to match same-value cards. They can be played either with one player as a memory test or with two players to see who can match pairs the quickest. These games can also be made more challenging by adding variations to the basic premise. Examples of card games in this category are Gin Rummy and Cribbage.

TRICK-TAKING GAMES

Trick-taking games are a little more intricate than some games in the other categories, so I'll explain them in terms of their similarities. Overall, these types of games essentially involve players having limits on the rounds of play and when everyone has put their cards down, a winner is determined based on the rules of the game. Within this category there are plain-trick, point-trick, and trick-and-draw games. Trick-taking games are more structured than other types of games, and therefore may be less accessible for everyone. However, they can be appealing for players looking for a challenge. Examples of games in this category include Spades and Whist.

VYING GAMES

With entire elaborate casinos built in their honor, vying games rely on players betting on who they think has the better hand. Players have to make the best decision they can based on the information they've observed during each hand of the game. These games often have an ideal balance of chance and skill. Though these games are associated with gambling, many people play for fun. The most obvious example of this category is Poker, which has its own long list of variations that some people may prefer. Blackjack is another popular example.

• • CARD GAME COMMON MISTAKES • •

In general, there are a few common mistakes that are best to avoid when playing card games. The following are three common ones.

PLAYING TOO FAST: Although it may feel good to play your cards as soon as you see an opportunity, many card games reward taking time to examine the current state and planning for what may be coming next. Being too eager can open yourself up to simple errors.

BEING TOO PASSIVE: On the other hand, it can also be detrimental to play too slowly. In competitive games, you want to balance your pacing so that you're thoughtful but efficient, without giving your opponent too much time to plan their moves against you.

NOT SHUFFLING THE DECK: This misstep can derail a game before it even starts. While shuffling is especially important when you play with a new deck of cards, it's also critical when you're playing with a deck you've used before, since the cards could be grouped by suit or value.

WINNING STRATEGIES

Every card game, even the simple ones, has some key strategies to keep in mind to increase your chances of winning. Even though winning isn't everything, it can make the experience more enjoyable when you're putting more intention into your moves. Although they might be hard to remember at first, with time and practice, you'll be able to master these winning strategies.

GIN RUMMY: While it is tempting to focus on the cards in your hand, you need to be mindful of the Discard pile when you play Gin Rummy. Before you discard something from your hand, think about what else you've seen discarded to know if something you need might still be within reach.

CRAZY EIGHTS: If you can change the suit after another player names one, it's likely a smart move, since they usually have some of that suit in their hand, even if they're trying to block other players by playing a different one. As such, keep any 8s in your hand for as long as possible so that you can use this strategy as needed.

BLACKJACK: When playing at a table, don't worry about what other players are or aren't doing. This is a game between you and the dealer, so focus on them and make smart decisions. Keeping a level head and sticking to the basic strategies will take you a long way.

CLASSIC SOLITAIRE: It is most important in this game to expose hidden cards, not to just empty piles for the sake of it. It's wise to focus on the pile with the most hidden cards and operate around that first.

WAR: While not thought of as a strategy game, there is no explicit rule in War about how cards are returned to the winner's deck. A winning method can be to order them in a pattern of "high, low, low" values to prepare for when the next "war" breaks out.

COMMON CARD LINGO

With a past as storied as the games themselves, card jargon and slang has evolved over the years. Here are definitions for some of the most important words for you to know.

CUT THE DECK: to halve the deck, usually after someone has shuffled

DEUCE: a number 2 value card of any suit

FACE CARD: one of the picture cards in a deck (a King, Queen, or Jack)

FOLLOW SUIT: to put down a card of the same suit as the lead suit

HAND: all the cards that a player has in their possession

HOLE CARD: a card that has been dealt into the game facedown

IN TURN: next to play in the given game (as of a player)

LEAD SUIT: set by the first card played; if the first player puts down a Jack of Spades, the lead suit is Spades

LEFT IN THE LURCH: a situation in which, due to game circumstances, a player is put into a hopeless or unwinnable position

PLAIN SUIT: a suit that is not assigned as a trump suit; also, may be used to refer to any card belonging to said suit

SHOWDOWN: the moment in which, after rounds of betting, the remaining players in a vying game show their hands to determine the winner

SPOT CARD: a card with a numeric value, as opposed to a face card

STOCK: the pile of cards left over once everyone is dealt into the game

TRUMP CARD: a specific card that has a special value that makes it greater than the other cards; a **"TRUMP SUIT"** is a suit assigned a greater value than the other suits

UPCARD: a card played on the table faceup

WILD CARD: a card that can be designated by the player to be any value or suit

• • A NOTE ON RULES • •

As I mentioned previously, many card games have roots that date back hundreds of years. With such a wide and varied history, the rules of all these games may be different to readers depending on their background or family customs. I will use the traditional default structure for each game as I highlight them, but I encourage everyone to put their own spin on each game they play. You may have heard the term "house rules" before, which describes a set of rules for a card game that is characteristic of a single household and may differ in someone else's house. Feel free to come up with your own "house rules," or try those of your friends.

However, some basic rules apply to all card games. These include not looking at the cards until they're dealt, always dealing to the left, and being kind to others who are just learning the game. We were all new to something once!

HOW TO USE THIS BOOK

This is the final housekeeping section before we get to the good stuff. Here, I'll explain how the book is organized and how you can use it. There is a very deliberate structure and flow to the parts and chapters, which will help you navigate the book and build your knowledge of card games.

Most notably, there are two parts to this book. The first focuses on solo games, including both strictly single-player Patience Games (chapter 1) and Solo Variations on Multiplayer Games (chapter 2). There is a total of 20 games in part 1. Part 2 gets into card games for two players. It can be difficult to find good games for only two players, so I've included 32 great options for you and a buddy. They are separated into Capturing, Shedding, Matching, Trick-Taking, and Vying (chapter 3 through chapter 7).

Within each category-based chapter, the games are organized by difficulty level. I've labelled them as easy, medium, or hard. Easy is defined as something anyone can quickly pick up and play (including children). Medium is defined as something not everyone can play right away, but can pick it up with a small amount of time and practice. Hard is defined as something not everyone can play right away and that requires a decent amount of practice to fully understand. You'll see entire categories that are harder than others, so use the difficulty levels to guide what games you want to try, depending on your goals.

Now that you know how to use this book, it's time to take out your deck. Let the games begin!

PART I

CARD GAMES FOR SOLO PLAYERS

CHAPTER 1

PATIENCE GAMES

CONCENTRATION

Concentration is a simple classic card game that is highly flexible and accessible to all players. It can be a great memory and matching activity for kids or simply something for adults to play to pass the time.

OBJECTIVE OF THE GAME: Match pairs of the same value cards until all pairs are found in the least number of turns

MATERIALS: One standard deck of cards with the Jokers removed

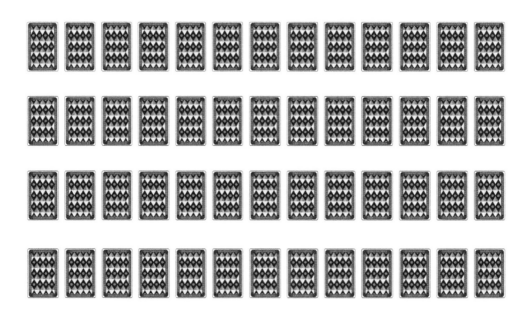

HOW TO DEAL:

Shuffle the deck and lay out the cards facedown in a grid of four rows with 13 cards each.

HOW TO PLAY:

While this game can be played with more players, there is a meditative, mindful quality to playing it on your own. Once the cards are set up, flip one card over and then another. If they're a value match (for example, two 5s or two 10s), then you take the pair. If they aren't, you must flip them both back over. You repeat these turns until all the pairs are found. You can measure your success by how many turns it takes to complete the game and how well you've been able to remember where the cards are as you go.

VARIATIONS:

Try finding value and color match pairs (such as the 3 of Hearts and the 3 of Diamonds), adding in another deck of cards for a longer game, or laying out the cards in a more intricate shape.

LEVEL OF DIFFICULTY: EASY

LENGTH OF PLAY: LESS THAN 5 MINUTES

ALTERNATIVE NAMES: KLONDIKE, PATIENCE

CLASSIC SOLITAIRE

With roots dating back to the 18th century, Solitaire has exploded in recent popularity due to its inclusion on many personal computers and smartphones.

OBJECTIVE OF THE GAME: Build up four stacks of cards starting with the Ace and ending with the King, with each stack being composed of a single suit

MATERIALS: One standard deck of cards with the Jokers removed

HOW TO DEAL:

Starting from left to right, place one card faceup, then deal one card facedown to make the other six columns. Continue by placing one card faceup on the second column, and then place five cards facedown on top of the remaining five columns. Keep this pattern going until the last column has one card faceup on top of six other cards that are facedown. This forms what is called the Tableau. The remaining cards form the hand that you pull from.

HOW TO PLAY:

There are four important play areas in Solitaire. The Tableau, the Foundations (where you create the whole suit piles), your hand, and the Discard pile (where you place cards that cannot be put on the Tableau).

You start each game by sorting any of the faceup cards in the Tableau, cascading cards down in descending face values (place a 9 on top of a 10, an 8 on top of a 9, and so on). Your stacks must also alternate colors (i.e., a 3 of Diamonds can go on a 4 of Clubs, but a 3 of Spades cannot). As you move cards out of a column, the next card in that column can be turned faceup. If you discover an Ace, place it in the Foundation to start one of the suit piles. If an empty column is created, you can move a King card over to it and then have lower face value cards descend from it in order.

Once you cannot make any more moves, you can start drawing one card at a time from your hand. If the card can be placed somewhere on the Tableau, then do so; if not, that card must go to the Discard pile, and you draw another card.

Keep this sequence going as you build out each column on the Tableau and fill the piles for each suit on the Foundations. If you get stuck, you can transfer all the Discard pile back to your hand and try to keep going, or you can start a new game.

VARIATIONS:

Try drawing every third card from the hand or creating more than seven columns.

LEVEL OF DIFFICULTY: MEDIUM

LENGTH OF PLAY: 5 TO 10 MINUTES

ALTERNATIVE NAMES: NONE

SPIDER SOLITAIRE

Originating in 1949, this game takes its name from the eight legs of a spider because there are eight Foundation piles to sort cards into.

OBJECTIVE OF THE GAME: Sort all the same suit cards in sequence from Ace to King in the Foundation

MATERIALS: Two standard decks of cards with the Jokers removed

HOW TO DEAL:

Create 10 stacks of cards, with each stack containing five cards; place the first four cards facedown, and the fifth card faceup.

HOW TO PLAY:

The play style of Spider Solitaire is very similar to Classic. You are still trying to create numeric stacks that alternate colors, but the stacks can be moved to reveal facedown cards underneath, and you are trying to build up your Foundations (this time with eight suits). However, when you pull cards from your hand, you place one card faceup on *all* the columns, and all the column spaces must be filled with at least one card prior to dealing more cards. This can either work for you or against you and makes this version of the game more challenging than the Classic version.

VARIATIONS:

Try playing with only one or two suits of cards versus all four or using four decks instead of two. The rules are the same in both cases, it just adds a different dynamic and length to the game.

LEVEL OF DIFFICULTY: MEDIUM

LENGTH OF PLAY: LESS THAN 5 MINUTES

ALTERNATIVE NAMES: NONE

EMPEROR

Another form of the classic version of Solitaire, Emperor expands the board by combining two decks.

OBJECTIVE OF THE GAME: Build all cards into their respective Foundations, of which there are eight total

MATERIALS: Two standard decks of cards with the Jokers removed

HOW TO DEAL:

Shuffle together the two packs of cards. Deal 40 cards into 10 columns of four cards each, with the three bottom cards facedown and the fourth faceup. Remaining cards are left facedown in the Stock pile.

HOW TO PLAY:

As with Classic or Spider Solitaire, you build up columns in descending numeric order and alternating colors, reveal cards by moving the top faceup cards out of the columns, and build up the Foundations from Ace to King (ascending order) for each suit. As in Classic Solitaire, you draw one card from your Stock pile at a time, and discard unused cards from the Stock pile to a separate Discard pile. However, in Emperor (unlike in Classic Solitaire), the top card of the Discard pile can still be played. Additionally, as spaces open on the Tableau, any card can be put in that column to build a stack, not just a King.

The game ends when there are no more moves to make or all the Foundations are built.

VARIATIONS:

Since Emperor itself is a slight variation on Classic Solitaire, there aren't any listed variations for Emperor.

LEVEL OF DIFFICULTY: MEDIUM

LENGTH OF PLAY: LESS THAN 5 MINUTES

ALTERNATIVE NAMES: IDLE YEAR,
TOWER OF BABEL

ACCORDION

A simple take on Solitaire, Accordion gets its name because the goal of the game is to stack the deck so that it looks like an accordion.

OBJECTIVE OF THE GAME: Stack the entire deck of cards into one pile

MATERIALS: One standard deck of cards with the Jokers removed

HOW TO DEAL:

Simply lay out the cards from the entire deck faceup in one straight line. Play can begin while the dealer is laying out the cards.

HOW TO PLAY:

In this game, you are meant to stack cards on top of other cards with the same value or suit. The catch is that you can only stack a card onto the card directly left of it, or onto the card that is placed three spaces to the left (if the cards are of the same suit or value). When cards start making a stack, the whole stack moves along with the top card being the marker of value to determine future moves.

One interesting aspect of this game is that you can play while the cards are being dealt or wait until they are all on the table. If you choose to stop the cards being laid out, you can still only move and stack cards to the left. Once you're done moving your cards, the dealing continues.

This is often another game that is hard to win but its relative simplicity means that it can be composed of quick rounds.

VARIATIONS:

One variation is to place a King and Queen on opposite ends of the line and try to bring them together by condensing all the other cards into piles beneath them.

LEVEL OF DIFFICULTY: MEDIUM

LENGTH OF PLAY: 5 TO 10 MINUTES

ALTERNATIVE NAMES: NONE

BAKER'S DOZEN

This game is basically a version of Classic Solitaire in which all the cards are visible and on the table!

OBJECTIVE OF THE GAME: Complete the four Foundational suited stacks of cards

MATERIALS: One standard deck of cards with the Jokers removed

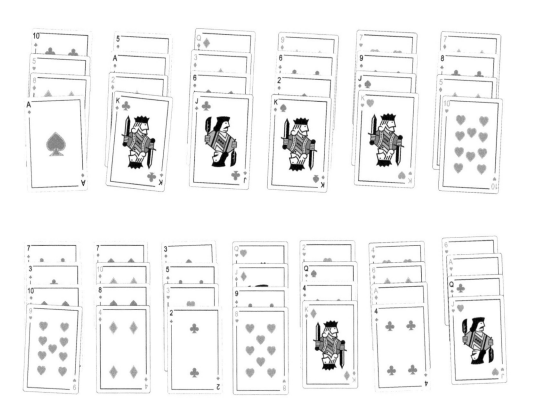

HOW TO DEAL:

Shuffle the deck and deal out 13 columns of 4 faceup cards each. Move the King cards to the bottom of their respective columns. Make spots for each of the four Foundation piles.

HOW TO PLAY:

Generally, this game plays like Classic Solitaire, but there are a few key differences. As in Solitaire, you are creating descending numeric stacks and trying to build up your Foundation. However, unlike in Solitaire, the suits and colors do not matter while stacking (i.e., a 3 of Clubs can go on top of a 4 of Spades), only the top card in a column can be moved (even if the cards are in sequence in the rest of the column), and once a column becomes empty during play, it must remain empty.

Once you've built each suit up from its Foundation in ascending order, the game is won. If you get stuck without any more possible moves, then you must start over.

VARIATIONS:

There is only a slight variation to this game: the Kings are not automatically moved to the bottoms of their columns but can be moved to empty spots.

PYRAMID

Named for the layout's resemblance to a pyramid, this game is an elaborate combination of luck, strategy, and math.

OBJECTIVE OF THE GAME: Match and remove all the cards from the pyramid, the Stock pile, and the Discard pile

MATERIALS: One standard deck of cards with the Jokers removed

HOW TO DEAL:

Shuffle the deck. Begin laying out the pyramid by setting one card down faceup, then two more on top faceup, then three faceup, continuing until 28 cards are dealt. The remaining cards are put facedown into a Stock pile.

HOW TO PLAY:

Once the table is set, you begin by moving pairs of uncovered cards (those that do not have any other cards resting on top of them) whose values equal 13 (Aces are worth 1, Jacks 10, Queens 11, Kings 12). Any pair that has been matched is removed from the game. As pairs are made, more cards are uncovered that can be matched. If you're stuck, you can draw a card from the Stock pile. If this card does not make a pair, then you move it to a Discard pile and continue drawing until an appropriate card appears. Discarded cards remain in play throughout the whole game. The top card from the Discard pile and the Stock pile can be combined if they equal 13. You can also combine a card from the Discard pile with a card in the pyramid. You've won once the pyramid, the Discard pile, and the Stock pile are all cleared.

VARIATIONS:

Try inverting your pyramid, not using a Stock pile at all, or setting aside a select few cards in a Reserve pile to use instead of Stock and Discard piles.

WISH SOLITAIRE

Rumor has it that if you remove all the cards in this game on your first try, you can make a wish come true!

OBJECTIVE OF THE GAME: Clear away all the pairs of same-value cards

MATERIALS: One standard deck of cards with all the 2-, 3-, 4-, 5-, and 6-value cards and Jokers removed

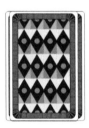

HOW TO DEAL:

You should be starting with 32 cards (Aces, 7s, 8s, 9s, 10s, Jacks, Queens, Kings) when you start dealing. Shuffle the cards and place four cards face-down in a pile. Then, repeat this to create eight total piles of cards (you don't need to shuffle each time).

HOW TO PLAY:

The premise is simple enough; you want two same-value cards to match, regardless of suit. You flip up the top card of each pile, find a match, and then flip the next card in the pile faceup. When you run out of matches, the game is over, and you can restart. The outcome of this game comes down to pure luck most of the time.

VARIATIONS:

There are no known variations of this game.

LA BELLE LUCIE

This is a simple and fun take on the classic setup of Solitaire. All you need is plenty of space on your table.

OBJECTIVE OF THE GAME: Build up each of the four foundations from Ace to King, one for each suit

MATERIALS: One standard deck of cards with the Jokers removed

HOW TO DEAL:

Shuffle the cards and lay out the entire deck in sets of three faceup. Each set of three should be splayed out so you can see all of them. One card will remain on its own.

HOW TO PLAY:

The only cards that can be moved are the ones at the top of each set. The basic rules of Solitaire apply here in terms of building up the Foundations. The only caveat being that with all the cards on the table, it can be harder to rearrange cards to reveal what you need. Also, you cannot fill empty space on the table to break up the sets.

VARIATIONS:

Fun variants allow a complete re-deal of all the remaining cards or one free move of any one card underneath other cards on the board.

TRIPEAKS SOLITAIRE

This card game combines elements from Pyramid and Golf Solitaire for a challenging but fun experience.

OBJECTIVE OF THE GAME: Transfer all the cards from the three-peaked Tableau to the Discard pile

MATERIALS: One standard deck of cards with the Jokers removed

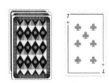

HOW TO DEAL:

Shuffle your deck and lay out three peaks composed of 30 cards total. The peaks are four cards high and all the cards on the first row are placed faceup. One card is turned up in the Discard pile, the rest of the 21 cards are put face-down in the Stock to use as needed.

HOW TO PLAY:

Cards can be moved from the peaks to the Discard pile if they are one less or one more than the value of the card currently on top. The cards can wrap from King to Ace, meaning you can build an Ace on a King and vice versa. The Discard pile can be continually built up or down and the suit doesn't matter. When both of the face-up cards covering the bottom of one of the face-down cards in the pyramid are removed, the face-down card can be turned face-up. If a card is needed because no movement is possible from the Tableau, one may be pulled from the Stock. If the Stock is gone and no other moves can be made, the game is over.

VARIATIONS:

There are no variants for this unique game.

LEVEL OF DIFFICULTY: HARD

LENGTH OF PLAY: LESS THAN 5 MINUTES

ALTERNATIVE NAME: CANFIELD SOLITAIRE

CANFIELD

This game is another Solitaire spinoff that was created in the 1890s. It was originally a casino game, since it has a very low probability of winning.

OBJECTIVE OF THE GAME: Move all the cards to the four Foundations by suit in an unexpected order

MATERIALS: One standard deck of cards with the Jokers removed

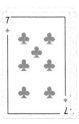    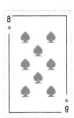

HOW TO DEAL:

Shuffle the deck, then deal 13 cards faceup to make the Reserve pile. Then deal one card for the first Foundation. The other three Foundations must match the value of the first card as they become available. For example, if the first Foundation card is a 4-value card, that is where that Foundation and the rest of the Foundations begin.

Start the Tableau by dealing four cards, with each card faceup. The rest of the cards go into the Stock pile facedown.

HOW TO PLAY:

After the setup is complete, the player begins by either pulling from the Reserve or moving any of the Tableau cards. The cards can be stacked in the Tableau in alternating colors and descending values, as in Classic Solitaire. Cards can also go from the Reserve straight to the Foundations. As with Classic Solitaire, columns can be moved altogether. Empty columns can also be filled by the Reserve.

If no cards from the Reserve can be played in an appropriate place, then cards from the Stock pile can be considered. Players can deal three cards at a time from the Stock pile (with only the third card active until it has been removed to uncover the second). Relevant drawn cards can be placed either in the Foundations or the Tableau; unplayable cards go to the Discard pile.

The game is finished when the player places all cards on the Foundations. This is highly unlikely, so sometimes players will adjust the goal to be more attainable.

VARIATIONS:

The variants are diverse when it comes to this game. One of them is Chameleon, in which the Reserve has 12 cards and there are only three columns in the Tableau. Super Canfield is played with the entire Reserve visible and any gaps in the Tableau can be filled by any card.

FORTY THIEVES

Rumored to be the game that Napoleon played during his exile, this popular version of two-deck Solitaire comes with a bit of added difficulty.

OBJECTIVE OF THE GAME: Move all the cards to the Foundations with their like suit, in ascending order

MATERIALS: Two standard decks of cards with the Jokers removed

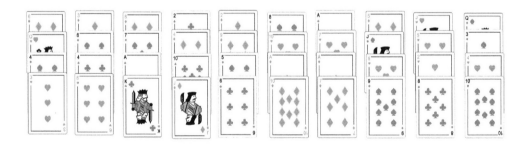

HOW TO DEAL:

For this game, deal 10 Tableau columns of four cards each. All cards should be faceup and visible. The remaining cards are left in the Stock pile. Make space for the eight Foundations.

HOW TO PLAY:

Forty Thieves is similar to Classic Solitaire in that the Foundations need to be built up in ascending order by suit, starting with the Ace. However, columns in the Tableau are built down by suit only (i.e., a 3 of Diamonds can only go on a 4 of Diamonds), and you can only move the top card from any Tableau column, not full descending stacks. Additionally, any card can fill an empty space.

You can take one card at a time from the Stock, and put it on the board appropriately, either in the Foundations or the Tableau. If it cannot be played, then it must be discarded into a Discard pile. You can use the top card from the Discard pile, but you can only go through the Stock once. It cannot be reset to keep playing the same game.

VARIATIONS:

Since Forty Thieves can be hard to play, variants have been developed that make it easier to win, such as dealing the Aces to the Foundations when starting the game.

LEVEL OF DIFFICULTY: HARD

LENGTH OF PLAY: 5 TO 10 MINUTES

ALTERNATIVE NAMES: NONE

DEVIL'S GRIP

This is a fascinating solo game with some very specific rules. It's definitely best for more experienced players.

OBJECTIVE OF THE GAME: Get each of the four sets built with as many of the cards in play and the least amount of cards leftover

MATERIALS: Two standard decks of cards with the Aces and Jokers removed

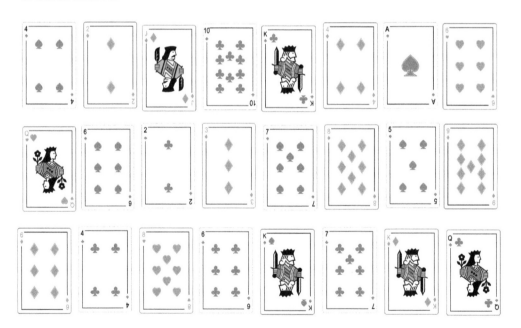

HOW TO DEAL:
Shuffle the decks and deal out three rows of eight cards, all faceup. The remaining cards will stay in the Stock pile, facedown.

HOW TO PLAY:
In Devil's Grip, cards can be stacked if they are the same suit and adhere to one of the following specific orders:

- 2, 5, 8, J
- 3, 6, 9, Q
- 4, 7, 10, K

You don't need to wait to have a complete sequence to start stacking cards, but the cards must be in one of the specific orders. Cards are meant to remain in their respective four card stacks. If you were to successfully complete the game, each of the four card stacks would maintain a three-by-eight grid. Also, any individual cards or stacks of cards in each row or column can be moved to open spaces at any time for your visual and organizational preferences.

When spaces open up as you stack, the top card from the Stock pile must be put down to replace it. If you are getting stuck, then you can deal out some cards from the Stock pile in sets of three, with the top card value being what the player can use, if possible. Unused cards go to a Discard pile, but the number of cards in the Discard pile count against a player's score at the end of the game. Scoring simply boils down to counting the number of cards left in the deck. The lower the score, the better your outcome.

If there are no more possible moves left, the game is over.

VARIATIONS:
The intricate rules of Devil's Grip have not inspired any popular variants.

LEVEL OF DIFFICULTY: HARD

LENGTH OF PLAY: LESS THAN 5 MINUTES

ALTERNATIVE NAMES: LAYING SIEGE, STREETS AND ALLEYS

BELEAGUERED CASTLE

This is another very difficult patience game that can be lost within just a few moves!

OBJECTIVE OF THE GAME: Have all the cards built into their suited Foundations in ascending order

MATERIALS: One standard deck of cards with the Jokers removed

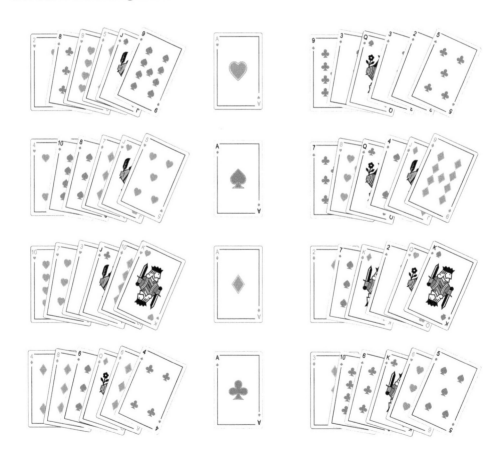

HOW TO DEAL:

First, remove the Aces from the deck and line them up vertically to form the Foundations. Then, deal one pile of six cards to the left of each Ace, and another pile of six cards to the right of each Ace. All cards should be faceup.

HOW TO PLAY:

The top card on each row can be moved to the Foundations or to a pile in another row. The piles are stacked based on ascending value, but suits are irrelevant. The Foundations, however, are built by suits in ascending order. If a space becomes empty, it can be filled with any card. Games can end quickly, just like with other patience games, if the layout of cards is simply not working in the player's favor.

VARIATIONS:

Common variants include using the Aces in the rows so that Foundations begin empty, choosing a different Foundation card to build up from, or giving the player a designated number of extra spaces to move cards around.

CHAPTER 2

SOLO VARIATIONS ON MULTIPLAYER GAMES

LEVEL OF DIFFICULTY: EASY

LENGTH OF PLAY: 5 TO 10 MINUTES

ALTERNATIVE NAME: TRASH

GARBAGE

This is a simple game of luck to play to pass the time. Try not to be stuck with too much "garbage" at the end of each round!

OBJECTIVE OF THE GAME: Complete a sequence of cards from Ace to 10

MATERIALS: One standard deck of cards with the Jokers removed

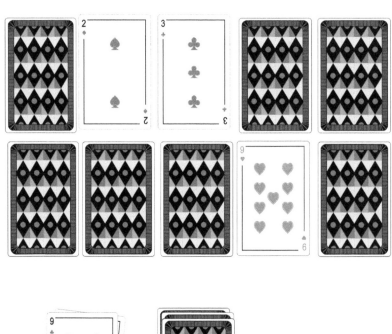

HOW TO DEAL:

Shuffle your deck and deal out 10 cards, facedown, in two rows of five. The rest of the cards can be placed in a facedown Stack pile for you to draw from.

HOW TO PLAY:

You begin play by drawing a card from the Stack. Depending on the numeric value of the card, you place that card in the corresponding spot in the rows, counting from left to right, top to bottom. You replace the facedown card with the card you just drew. For example, if your first card drawn is a 7, then you would count to the seventh card in the rows, swapping it out with the face-down card that is there.

Then, you repeat the process with whatever the numeric value is of the card now in your hand. If the card is already played or is a face card (Jack, Queen, King), then you must discard it and draw from the Stock pile until you find all the necessary numeric value cards from Ace to 10.

If you get stuck, you can play additional rounds, by resetting the cards in the two rows but removing one card from the rows until you get to just the Ace. All the other rules stay the same. After you complete each round, count up the cards you discarded. You want to have the fewest cards discarded as possible. You can also track to see how quickly you completed each round and/or all the rounds together.

VARIATIONS:

The biggest variant you can try is to make one of the face cards into a wild card that can be placed in any number spot in your rows that hasn't been filled in yet.

GOLF SOLITAIRE

This is a game of speed that stays fresh because of how quickly it runs.

OBJECTIVE OF THE GAME: Transfer cards from the seven columns into the Discard pile as quickly as you can

MATERIALS: One standard deck of cards with the Jokers removed

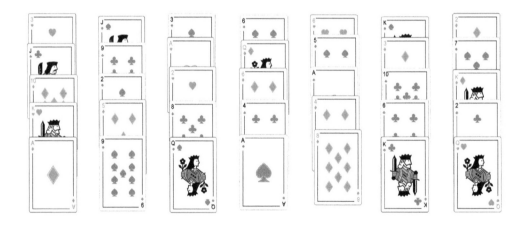

HOW TO DEAL:

Shuffle your deck and deal out seven columns of five faceup cards overlapping one another. The rest of the cards go facedown in a Stock pile. You should also have space in your play area for your Discard pile.

HOW TO PLAY:

All the cards at the bottom of each column are open to play. Your goal is to build a sequence of cards in the Discard pile in ascending or descending value regardless of suit. For example, when the game begins, if you have a 5 card at the bottom of one of the columns, you could pull that to put in your Discard pile, and then you need to find a 4 or a 6 next, then continue going from there until you cannot find another neighboring value card. Kings can be built on Aces, and Aces can be built on Kings.

If you can't build from the columns, you must pull a card from the Stock pile. The goal is to clear all the columns as quickly as possible, but if you clear the Stock pile and are still stuck, you lose the game.

This game balances skill and luck, with the former simply built by practicing your ability to move quickly and think several moves ahead.

VARIATIONS:

There are various ways to play this game including one in which you have six columns of six cards each and one in which you cannot "turn corners," meaning you cannot build on Kings with Aces or build on Aces with Kings. You can also combine these two variations.

IDIOT

The solo version of this game can give as much or as little entertainment as you wish since it can be played more or less without end.

OBJECTIVE OF THE GAME: Get the Ace of each suit at the bottom of each pile

MATERIALS: One standard deck of cards with the Jokers removed

HOW TO DEAL:
Shuffle your deck and make space in your play area for four piles and a Discard pile. All the cards remain in your hand when the game begins.

HOW TO PLAY:
Lay down four cards faceup next to one another to begin the four piles. If cards of the same suit appear, discard all but the highest card of that suit, putting them at the bottom of your hand (Aces rank high in this game). Replace the discarded cards with another card from the top of your hand. The purpose of this is so that each pile has a card of a different suit. Lay down four cards faceup on top of the existing ones. Continue laying down cards like this until you run out. If you ever have an empty pile, you can take the top card off a different pile and place it on the empty pile.

It is hard to lose this game on your own, so it is more about how long you want to keep at it. It is purely a game of luck as a solo endeavor.

VARIATIONS:
No variations of the solo version of this game exist.

CANASTA

Best suited for more experienced players, Canasta is from the Rummy family of card games and is popular the world over. This single player version trims down the core version of the game, which is typically played with four players.

OBJECTIVE OF THE GAME: Meld as many sets of three or more cards of the same value together as possible

MATERIALS: One standard deck of cards, Jokers included

HOW TO DEAL:

Shuffle the deck and deal yourself 11 cards. Place the rest of the cards in a facedown pile with the top card of the pile turned faceup beside it. If a Joker, 2, or 3 is turned over, then flip over another card on top of it.

HOW TO PLAY:

Play involves three steps: draw, meld if possible, and discard. The player typically draws the top card from the Stock pile but may draw the top card from the Discard pile if that card can be used to make a meld. Melds consist of at least three cards total with at least two natural cards (meaning not wild cards) of the same rank (e.g., three 7s). Wild cards (2s or Jokers) can be used to supplement melds so it is wise to hold onto them.

A canasta is a type of meld made from four natural cards. Once the player has made any possible melds they must place a card onto the Discard pile faceup. Then they continue drawing, melding, and discarding.

To track their success, the player may score their melds. Jokers are worth 50 points; Aces and 2s are worth 20 points; Kings, Queens, Jacks, 10s, 9s, and 8s are worth 10 points; 7s, 6s, 5s, 4s, and black 3s are worth 5 points; and red 3s are worth 100 points.

VARIATIONS:

Since this is a big deviation from the core game, there aren't any clear variations of the solo version of Canasta.

LEVEL OF DIFFICULTY: MEDIUM

LENGTH OF PLAY: 5 MINUTES OR FEWER

ALTERNATIVE NAME: CRIBBAGE SQUARE
SOLITAIRE

CRIBBAGE SQUARES

Based on the old English pub game, Cribbage Squares is a solo twist to test your foresight on different combinations of hands of cards.

OBJECTIVE OF THE GAME: Score as many points as you can with each of your various hand combinations

MATERIALS: One standard deck of cards with the Jokers removed

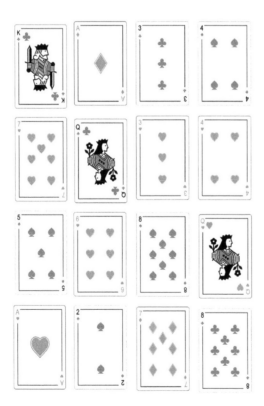
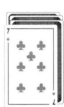

HOW TO DEAL:

Shuffle the deck and clear an area for a four-by-four square of cards. One by one, lay 16 cards faceup to form the grid. The order of the cards matters in this game (see the hand scoring guidelines that follow), so the player may lay them down in whatever open spot they choose. The rest of the cards form the Stock, and the top card is laid faceup. This top card is known as the Starter.

HOW TO PLAY:

Each of the four columns and rows form a five-card cribbage hand with the fifth card being the Starter. Each hand is scored individually and your final score for the round is the sum of all eight scores. The scoring in this game is a bit complex, but here's the breakdown:

- A distinct pair of matching cards scores 2 points

- 3 or more matching cards score 1 point

- A distinct pair of matching cards whose values added together total 15 or more scores 2 points (face cards all count for 10, Aces count for 1)

- Four or five cards all the same suit counts for 5 points

- A Jack in your hand that is the same suit as the Starter is called a "Nob" and scores 1 extra point

- A Starter that is a Jack automatically scores 2 points

Once you've tallied up your scores, you can shuffle the cards, reset, and play again to see if you can beat your personal best.

VARIATIONS:

The variations here involve the use of or the exclusion of reserves. With no reserves, the game is much more about luck, but with one or two five-card reserves available to draw from and play into the square, there is an opportunity for more skill.

POKER SQUARES

For lovers of Poker, this game offers a fun solo version to test your understanding and ability to plan for different Poker hand combinations.

OBJECTIVE OF THE GAME: Score as many points with your various hands as possible

MATERIALS: One standard deck of cards with the Jokers removed

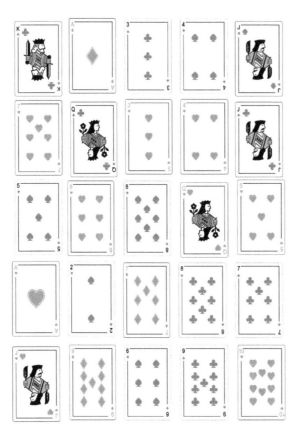

HOW TO DEAL:

Shuffle the deck and prepare a play space for a five-by-five square of cards. One by one, deal 25 cards faceup to form the grid. The order of the cards matters in this game (see the hand scoring guidelines that follow), so the player may lay them down in whatever open spot they choose.

HOW TO PLAY:

Each of the five columns and rows count as a hand. Each hand is scored individually and your final score for the round is the sum of all 10 Poker hands. The scoring is as follows:

- Royal flush (an Ace, King, Queen, Jack, and 10 all the same suit) = 100 points

- Straight flush (five consecutive value cards of the same suit) = 75 points

- Four of a kind (four cards of the same value) = 50 points

- Full house (three cards of the same rank plus a pair) = 25 points

- Flush (any five cards of the same suit) = 20 points

- Straight (any five consecutive value cards not of the same suit) = 15 points

- Three of a kind (three cards of the same rank) = 10 points

- Two pairs (two pairs of same value cards of any suit) = 5 points

- One pair (one pair of same value cards of any suit) = 2 points

For the hands where there are leftover cards (three of a kind leaves two odd cards leftover, two pairs leaves one odd card leftover, etc.), the other cards in the hand can be anything. Also, it is always good to remember that Aces can be played as a high or low card in the hands that require a run of consecutive value cards.

VARIATIONS:

For one variation, also score the two hands along the diagonals.

PART II

CARD GAMES FOR TWO PLAYERS

CHAPTER 3

CAPTURING GAMES

BEGGAR MY NEIGHBOR

This children's card game originated in the mid-1800s in England and can be played with two to four players.

OBJECTIVE OF THE GAME: Win all the cards

MATERIALS: One standard deck of cards with the Jokers removed

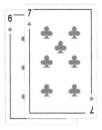

HOW TO DEAL:

Shuffle the deck and deal out all the cards evenly between the players. The respective decks are placed facedown in front of each player.

HOW TO PLAY:

Players take turns drawing the top card from their deck and placing it faceup in a central pile, alternating until a face card or Ace is played (also known as "court cards"). The type of court card played determines the opposing player's action:

- Ace: four cards are played, laid down one at a time
- King: three cards are played, laid down one at a time

- Queen: two cards are played, laid down one at a time
- Jack: one card is played

As the cards are being laid down, if another court card is played, then the process resets according to the new court card and moves to the next player to play all their necessary cards. If all the cards played are numeric, then the player who laid down the initial court card takes all the cards in the center. Play then resumes normally with the next player in the group.

If any player runs out of cards, then they're knocked out. Games of Beggar My Neighbor can go on for a while given the pure luck of the game, so feel free to determine the winner based on who has the most cards after a preset amount of time.

VARIATIONS:

No variations of this game exist, but it does share a lot of similarities to other capturing games.

GO FISH

This classic game is great for kids or adults and can be played with two to five players.

OBJECTIVE OF THE GAME: Capture as many "books" of four like-value cards as possible

MATERIALS: One standard deck of cards with the Jokers removed

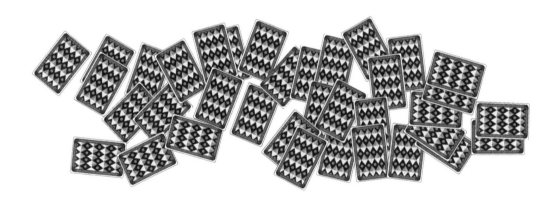

HOW TO DEAL:

Shuffle the deck and deal seven cards to each player. The remaining cards are placed facedown and spread out across the table to form the "ocean."

HOW TO PLAY:

Play begins with the first player (whoever isn't the dealer) asking the other player if they have a particular value card (suit doesn't matter). If the other player has the card asked for, they must give it to the asker. If the other player doesn't have the card asked for, then the asker must "go fish" and pick a card randomly from the ocean. Play then moves to the asked player and continues in this fashion.

The goal is to create books of four cards with the same value, so if a player achieves this, they must place the book faceup in front of them so the other player can see. If a player runs out of cards in their hand at any time, then they can pick up a card from the ocean if there are cards available. Otherwise, their play has ended.

The game fully ends when all 13 books are created. The winner is the one with the most books.

VARIATIONS:

Go Fish has a number of slight variations. Try fishing for pairs instead of books, playing with multiple decks, or including the Jokers.

LEVEL OF DIFFICULTY: EASY

LENGTH OF PLAY: 10 TO 20 MINUTES

ALTERNATIVE NAMES: SLAPS,
HEART ATTACK

SLAPJACK

This is a fun, simple, and active card game that shares many similarities with Beggar My Neighbor and can be played with two to four players.

OBJECTIVE OF THE GAME: Obtain all the cards

MATERIALS: One standard deck of cards with the Jokers removed

HOW TO DEAL:

Shuffle the deck and split it evenly between the players.

HOW TO PLAY:

Players alternate drawing a card from their deck and playing it faceup in the center of the table. When a Jack is played, both players must try to be the first to physically slap the card. The first to do so takes the entire pile, shuffles it, and incorporates it at the bottom of their deck, thereby getting closer to winning all the cards. Play then resumes normally.

To prevent their opponent from slapping the Jack, a player may also simply play another card immediately on top of their Jack (no slapping necessary!). If this is done, no one takes the cards and play continues normally until the next Jack.

If a player runs out of cards, they can remain in play until the next Jack. If they slap the Jack, then they get all the cards and are back in the game. If they fail, then they're out of the game. The winner is the person who has all the cards. Alternatively, you can set a time limit and name the player who has the most cards when time is up as the winner.

VARIATIONS:

Sometimes, players will require that "Slapjack" be yelled when claiming the central pile. In this version, players can try to trick each other by yelling "Slapjack" when a card other than a Jack has been played. If the opposing player is tricked into slapping the deck, the pile goes to the trickster.

WAR

This fierce two-player game of luck is quick to set up and fun to pass the time since no decisions must be made.

OBJECTIVE OF THE GAME: Collect all the cards

MATERIALS: One standard deck of cards with the Jokers removed

HOW TO DEAL:

Shuffle the deck and distribute it evenly between the two players. Leave each deck facedown in front of each player.

HOW TO PLAY:

Simultaneously, players turn over the top card of their deck and determine which card has the highest value. If a player's card has the higher value, then they take both cards and add them to the bottom of their deck. Players then continue revealing cards as before.

If the values match, then a "war" is declared. Each player lays out three cards facedown and a fourth faceup. Players compare the fourth card, known as their "war card." The player with the higher value card takes their war card, the opponent's war card, and the original two cards that started the war. They then incorporate them into their deck. If the two cards match in value, then the players overturn their third, second, and first cards as necessary until a victor emerges. The victor then takes all the cards that were put into play for the various wars, plus the original two, for a maximum of 10 cards.

Game play continues until one player has all the cards and the other has none.

VARIATIONS:

There are interesting variants on War, such as Peace, where the lower card always wins, or a version in which someone can steal victory during a war sequence if one of their three played cards is a Jack.

KNACK

This unique Swedish card game is played with fewer cards than your standard card game but still creates a dynamic playing experience. I've adapted some of the game rules to better fit in a modern card deck.

OBJECTIVE OF THE GAME: Best other players' hands by obtaining same-suit and high-value cards

MATERIALS: One standard deck of cards with the Jokers, 2s, 3s, 4s, 5s, and 6s removed (this should result in a 32-card deck). The values for the remaining cards are as follows: 7s, 8s, 9s, and 10s are all worth their numerical values. Jacks, Queens, and Kings all are worth 11 points. Aces are worth 12 points.

HOW TO DEAL:

The dealer gives themself and the other player three cards facedown and then deals themself one more hand of three facedown cards. After looking at the first hand (but not the second), the dealer chooses to either keep their hand or swap for the second hand, trying to maximize the point value of their hand (see the scoring guidelines that follow). They then take the rejected hand and place it faceup in the center of the table.

HOW TO PLAY:

Once the initial hands are settled, the non-dealer player can do one of three things: swap one card from their hand with one card in the center of the table, swap all their cards with the cards in the center of the table, or pass and do nothing. They cannot swap two cards.

If the player passes, then the cards at the center are all replaced with new faceup cards. The players then both reveal their hands to see who wins the round. Hands are scored in one of two ways:

- If the player has three of a kind (three cards of the same value), they are scored by the sum of those values.

- If the player has two or three cards of the same suit, they are scored by the sum of those values.

To this end, the best hand is three Aces for 36 points. If at any time during the game, a player has an Ace and two (11-point) face cards, they win the round and must immediately show their hand. Once a hand is over, shuffle and reset all the players' hands. Play for as many hands as desired.

VARIATIONS:

There are a bunch of interesting variations of this game. Try looking up Dutch 31, Hosa Aba, 41, or Tri Palki.

CASSINO

Dating back to the late 1700s, Cassino is best played by two players and features an intricate set of rules. And, no, the name is not a typo!

OBJECTIVE OF THE GAME: Gather as many cards as you can to score more points than your opponent

MATERIALS: One standard deck of cards with the Jokers removed.

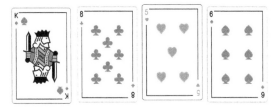

HOW TO DEAL:

The dealer shuffles the deck and deals out four cards to each player and four cards in the middle between the players. The rest of the deck is put to the side as Stock.

HOW TO PLAY:

Face cards have no value in the game and Aces = 1. Players alternate turns, each taking one of the four following actions:

- Trail = Discard one card faceup on the table.

- Pair = Use any card in your hand to take one or more same-value cards that are faceup on the table (e.g., taking a 2 with a 2).

- Combine = Use a number card in your hand to take two or more cards that add up to the value of the card used to take them (e.g., taking a 2 and a 4 with a 6 card).

- Build = Place a card on top of a faceup card and announce that you're building the sum value of the two cards (e.g., place a 3 on a 6 and announcing you're "building a 9").

Please note that building is only possible when a player has the same value card in their hand as the card they are placing it on. Builds can also be paired; these are called "multiple builds." For example, if you have a 9 in your hand, you can pair it with a 9-build made up of a 6 and a 3. This must happen on different turns, however.

Also note that because face cards have no value in the game, they can only be paired with each other one at a time.

Play continues to alternate between the players, with more cards dealt from the Stock to the players as their hands are emptied. Cards are not dealt from the Stock onto the table. The only way more cards can be put onto the table is for the players to discard them.

continued

The game is over when the Stock is all played and/or the last possible action is taken. Players then gather all their captures and score them as follows:

- Most cards = 3 points
- Most Spades = 1 point
- 10 of Diamonds = 2 points

- 2 of Spades = 1 point
- Each Ace = 1 point
- Clearing the board (known as a "sweep") = 1 point per sweep

The highest score wins! Any cards that were not captured do not factor into any player's score.

VARIATIONS:

There are numerous variations of this game, all unique and complex. Do an online search for Royal Cassino, Pluck Cassino, Portuguese Cassino, or California Cassino for some fresh new game rules.

CHAPTER 4

SHEDDING GAMES

OLD MAID

With a history dating back to the 1800s, this game is a simple classic known the world over. Perfect for an impromptu and quick activity, Old Maid can be played with just two players or up to 12 players!

OBJECTIVE OF THE GAME: Do not be left with the odd card at the end of the game once all the other cards have been paired

MATERIALS: One standard deck of cards with one card (typically a Queen) removed

HOW TO DEAL:

After removing a card and hiding it away, the dealer shuffles the deck and deals the cards until they're gone.

HOW TO PLAY:

Once the cards are all dealt, each player reviews their hand and finds any pairs of cards they have. Players cannot match three cards at a time, only pairs. Players then remove any pairs from their hand and place them facedown. The first player to go will offer their hand facedown to the neighbor on their left, who must choose one card at random to add to their hand. This cycle is repeated until all the pairs are made, leaving one player with the odd card.

VARIATIONS:

Several different countries have unique names for this game, but the core concept is the same: remove a card and the one left with the odd card is the loser.

KINGS CORNER

A unique and dynamic game, Kings Corner combines elements of Solitaire with classic shedding rules.

OBJECTIVE OF THE GAME: Play all your cards into the middle of the table before your opponent and have the least number of points at the end of the agreed-upon number of rounds

MATERIALS: One standard deck of cards with the Jokers removed

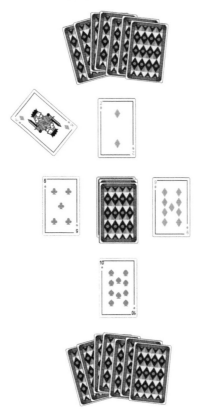

HOW TO DEAL:

Deal out seven cards to each player. The remaining cards are placed in the middle of the table. A card is taken from this deck and turned faceup on each side of the deck. If a King is uncovered during this phase, move it to a corner of the deck and pull another card to put down instead.

HOW TO PLAY:

Play begins each turn with the player drawing a card from the middle deck. Then, each player can play as many cards as they can or want to each turn. Cards are stacked around the middle deck in descending order and opposite suits, just like in Solitaire. Any King that is drawn during play is put at the corner of the middle deck.

Open spaces can be filled with any card. If the middle deck empties, play continues without players drawing new cards.

When the first person empties their hand, the other player tallies up their score depending on how many cards they have in their hand. Kings are worth 10 points and all other cards are worth 1 point each. This game is meant to be played in multiple rounds to see who ends up with the most points. The goal is to have the least number of points at the end of the agreed-upon number of rounds.

VARIATIONS:

There are no known variations to this game.

SPEED

This classic two-player game is simple in premise and, as the name implies, is all about fast-paced play.

OBJECTIVE OF THE GAME: Be the first player to get rid of all your cards

MATERIALS: One standard deck of cards with the Jokers removed

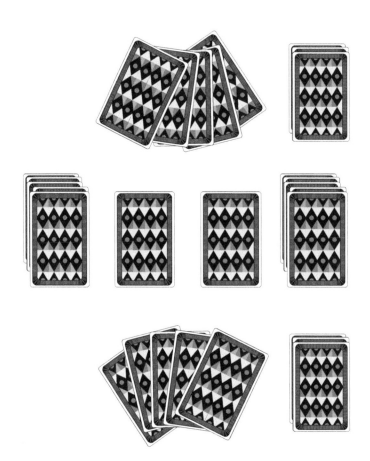

HOW TO DEAL:

Each player gets five cards dealt to them for their hand as well as a stack of 15 cards facedown for their personal Draw pile. Then, in the middle of the table, deal out two cards facedown next to each other. On the left and right of these two cards, deal out two five-card piles facedown.

HOW TO PLAY:

Once play begins, it is an ongoing game without specific turns. Each player's moves are happening simultaneously. To begin, each player turns over one of the single cards in the middle of the table. Then, they must play a card that is of a neighboring value to either of the cards that are faceup. Both players can work off either pile. Once a card is played, players must take a card from their personal Draw pile. There should be no more than five cards in a player's hand at a time.

Aces are high or low in this game, which allows for a continuous loop of cards in the piles. If neither player can put down a card, then a new card can be placed from the adjacent piles in the middle of the table.

Play to see who's the best out of three or five rounds of the game, since each round can go quite fast.

VARIATIONS:

There are many variations of this game. Examples include simply having the Jokers in the decks as wild cards or requiring the winning player to smack the table and say "Speed" as soon as they've emptied their hand. Spit is also a popular variant that has its own set of involved rules, so do an online search for Spit if you like Speed.

LEVEL OF DIFFICULTY: EASY

LENGTH OF PLAY: 5 TO 10 MINUTES

ALTERNATIVE NAME: GARBAGE

TRASH

Building on the single-player version of this game (called Garbage; see page 34), two-player Trash is a fun competition of speed, skill, and luck to see who can build their deck of 10 cards first.

OBJECTIVE OF THE GAME: Fill out your sequence of 10 cards before your opponent

MATERIALS: One standard deck of cards with the Jokers removed

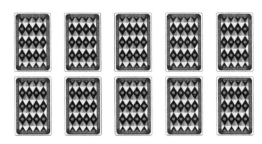

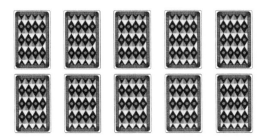

HOW TO DEAL:

In a large game area, lay out a grid of 10 facedown cards made up of two rows of five cards each in front of each player. The rest of the cards form the Stock pile in the middle of the table.

HOW TO PLAY:

The rules are the same as the single-player version of this game. The only change is that since there are two players, each one takes turns drawing from the deck and then placing the card in ascending sequence on their grid, with Aces counting as 1, 2s through 10s counting as their face value, Jacks being wild, and Queens as well as Kings being unplayable. The Ace is placed in the top left position on the grid, the 2 placed next, then the three, and so on.

Any duplicate or unplayable cards are put faceup in a Discard pile. When players draw their cards, they can choose to take it from the Stock or Discard pile.

This can be also be scored as best of three or best of five, since it is a game that is mostly about luck with a small bit of skill that can go relatively quickly.

VARIATIONS:

There are no variations of this game.

IDIOT

Playing cards that are equal to or superior in value to the card at the center of the table, players are trying to not be the last person with cards, otherwise known as the "Idiot."

OBJECTIVE OF THE GAME: Try not to be the last person to play all the cards in your hand

MATERIALS: One standard deck of cards with the Jokers removed

HOW TO DEAL:

Each player is given three cards laid out separately facedown, then three more cards faceup on top of each of the other three cards, then finally, they get three cards for their hand. The rest of the deck is put facedown in the middle of the table to form the Draw pile.

HOW TO PLAY:

At the start of the game, any player can swap any of the cards from their hand with the faceup cards in front of them. They are not required to make a swap. Once everyone has made their decision to swap (or not), the game begins.

Whichever player has the lowest value card in their hand starts the game by putting that card into the Discard pile. This can be determined simply by each player calling out the value of their lowest card. That player must draw another card from the Draw pile to maintain three cards in their hand. Then, the next player needs to try to play a card of equal or superior value to the value of the card on top of the Discard pile. Two or more cards of the same rank can be played together. If a player does not have any cards to play, they must pick up the entire Discard pile and put it in their hand. They will not draw cards until their hand returns to less than three cards.

In this game, the value of cards goes from Aces being highest to 3s being the lowest, 2s are wild, and 10s are burn cards. Any card can be played on top of a 2, and 10s will remove the entire Discard pile from play. When the Discard pile is removed, the next player can play any card they want. Another way to remove the Discard pile is by playing four of a kind all at once.

continued

Once the Draw pile is depleted and players are also clearing their hand, they begin to play the cards laid out in front of them from the start of the game. The faceup cards must be played first before playing the facedown cards. The facedown cards are played blindly, and if the card isn't of the proper value, that player must take the Discard pile and get through their hand again before getting back to their remaining facedown cards.

The premise of this game is simple in theory but does combine a good bit of luck and skill, so you can try to strategize better each time you play. Ultimately, however, luck can either help or hinder you.

VARIATIONS:

The only variation you could make to this game is changing which cards are wild and/or burn cards.

CRAZY EIGHTS

Dating back to the 1930s, this game has had international appeal, with various rule sets that can keep the game fresh each time it is played.

OBJECTIVE OF THE GAME: Be the first player to empty your hand

MATERIALS: One standard deck of cards with the Jokers removed

continued

HOW TO DEAL:

Seven cards are dealt to each player. The remaining cards are put facedown as the Draw pile. Then, the top card from that deck is drawn and turned faceup to create the Discard pile and to begin play.

HOW TO PLAY:

Each player takes turns discarding a card from their hand that either matches the face value of the card currently faceup in the Discard pile, is any 8 card, or is any club suit card. If no card in their hand can be used, the player must take cards from the Draw pile until they can discard one.

When an 8 is played, that player can declare that the next card put down by the other player must be a particular suit of their choosing.

If the Stock pile is depleted, then the Discard pile can be used to replenish it, keeping the top card to continue play. When a player empties their hand, they win the game. It is easy to then reset the game and play again by collecting all the cards, shuffling the deck, and dealing out the cards to each player's hand.

VARIATIONS:

You can include more special cards to the core game, such as having Queens skip the other player's turn, having Aces reverse direction, and/or having 2s force the other player to draw two cards. Generally, this is a very easy game to modify.

NERTS

Essentially a competitive version of Solitaire between two players, Nerts has roots reported back to the 1890s in the United Kingdom.

OBJECTIVE OF THE GAME: Be the first player to clear your "Nerts" pile

MATERIALS: Two standard decks of cards, one for each player, with the Jokers removed

continued

HOW TO DEAL:

Preferably each player's deck has a unique design to distinguish it. Each player shuffles their own deck and deals themselves four faceup cards to form their personal Tableau. Then, they create their Nerts pile by dealing 13 cards face-down in a pile next to the Tableau. Flip the top card of the Nerts pile face-up. The remaining cards of their deck make their own Stock pile.

HOW TO PLAY:

Play happens simultaneously in this game, so it requires quick reflexes and awareness of the whole play area to succeed. To empty their Nerts pile, players want to use the face-up card and flip the next card face-up for use. To do this, the player must add the face-up card either to their Tableau (sometimes called the "River"), where cards are stacked as in Solitaire (descending order, alternating colors), or to the central common area (sometimes called the "Lake"), where cards are stacked in ascending order, alternating colors. In order to play the face-up Nerts card, players may need to use their Stock (sometimes called the "Stream"). Cards are drawn from the Stock three at a time, as in Solitaire, and can be added to either their Tableau or the common area. Whole stacks of cards can be moved together, and an empty Tableau place can be filled with either the face-up Nerts card or a Stock card.

There is a good deal of strategy in this game. If you keep your cards in your own space, you risk taking too long to clear out your Nerts pile, but if you use the common area, you risk helping your opponent get rid of cards. Whoever clears their Nerts pile first wins, and the loser can assess how well they did by how many remaining Nerts cards they have (the fewer the better).

VARIATIONS:

There are no variations to this game.

CHAPTER 5

MATCHING GAMES

LEVEL OF DIFFICULTY: EASY

LENGTH OF PLAY: 5 TO 10 MINUTES

ALTERNATIVE NAMES: LEMON, ATLANTIS, CHANHASSEN

JAMES BOND

This game is perfect for two players to jump into quickly and easily and have a lot of fun. The way the game works can help with your memory, reflexes, and awareness. What this game has to do with James Bond is unknown.

OBJECTIVE OF THE GAME:
Be the first to build six piles of four-of-a-kind matches

MATERIALS: One standard deck of cards with the Jokers removed

HOW TO DEAL:

Shuffle the deck and lay out four cards faceup in between the two players. Then, lay out a row of six piles of four cards each facedown in front of each player.

HOW TO PLAY:

Gameplay is pretty simple: Each player takes one of their six piles of four cards and tries to swap a card at a time with one of the middle four faceup cards, with the goal of creating four-of-a-kind matches in each of your six piles. You can only hold one pile of four cards at a time, and once you create a matched pile, it is turned faceup.

Play in this game is simultaneous, and there must always be four cards in the middle and four cards in each pile.

VARIATIONS:

There are no major variations to this game, though you could allow players to swap more than one card at a time from the middle.

CANASTA

Although typically played with two teams of two players each, there are simple modifications that can be made to the game rules that allow two players to play against each other.

OBJECTIVE OF THE GAME: Make as many points as you can through melding same-value cards

MATERIALS: Two standard decks of cards with the Jokers included

HOW TO DEAL:

Each player is dealt 15 cards. The remaining cards are put into the middle of the table facedown in a pile for each player to draw from. If a player is dealt any red 3s, that player must put them faceup in front of them and draw a replacement card (or cards).

HOW TO PLAY:

One card from the Draw pile is turned over faceup to begin the game. If this card is a wild card (2s or Jokers) or a red 3, then another card is placed on top of it from the Draw pile.

Play involves three steps each turn: draw; meld, if possible; and discard. Players draw two cards at a time from the Stock pile. Players discard one card at a time to end their turn. They can also draw the top card from the Discard pile, only if that card can be used to make a meld.

Players make melds by matching at least three cards total with at least two natural cards (meaning not wild cards) of the same face value (e.g., three 7s). A canasta is a type of meld made from four natural cards.

Different card-value melds are worth various points. Jokers are worth 50 points; Aces and 2s are worth 20 points; Kings, Queens, Jacks, 10s, 9s, and 8s are worth 10 points; 7s, 6s, 5s, 4s, and black 3s are worth 5 points; and red 3s are worth 100 points.

When playing with two players, you can simply play up to a certain total point threshold, or for longer games, play until the Draw pile is exhausted and all possible melds are made.

VARIATIONS:

If you want to shake up the game, do an online search for the various international versions of this game from places like Brazil, Bolivia, or Italy.

LEVEL OF DIFFICULTY: MEDIUM

LENGTH OF PLAY: 5 TO 10 MINUTES

ALTERNATIVE NAMES: NONE

EGYPTIAN RAT SCREW

A simple game of luck, albeit with an odd name, that is well-suited for two players to test their reflexes.

OBJECTIVE OF THE GAME: Win all the cards

MATERIALS: One standard deck of cards with the Jokers removed

HOW TO DEAL:

Shuffle the deck and deal out all the cards in the deck between the two players. Cards remain in their pile facedown throughout play.

HOW TO PLAY:

Each player alternates placing the card from the top of their pile faceup in between them. If the card has a numerical value, play continues. If the card is a face card or an Ace, then the other player has to try to also play a face card or an Ace. Each different face card or Ace yields a different number of chances for the other player to find a face card or Ace: an Ace yields 4 chances, a King three, a Queen two, and a Jack 1. If all the chances are gone, then the last player to play the face card or Ace takes the entire pile of cards and adds them to the bottom of their deck.

Additionally, other special card combinations give any player the chance to slap the deck and take all the cards. These combinations are:

- Doubles (matching value cards)
- Sandwich (matching value cards played with one card in between)
- Top bottom (the top card of the pile has the same suit or value of the bottom card)
- Sequence of four (a cascade of sequential cards)
- Marriage (a King and Queen are played back-to-back)

If an opportunity for a slap is missed, then play continues. If there is a mistaken slap, there is a penalty of two cards that must be put into the middle pile.

VARIATIONS:

There are no known variations of this game.

LEVEL OF DIFFICULTY: MEDIUM

LENGTH OF PLAY: 5 TO 10 MINUTES

ALTERNATIVE NAMES: CANES, CASH, KENT

KEMPS

A much newer card game, Kemps is typically played with teams of two, but with some slight adjustments, you can make it fun for two players who want to face off.

OBJECTIVE OF THE GAME: Build four of a kind in your hand before your opponent

MATERIALS: One standard deck of cards with the Jokers removed

HOW TO DEAL:

Each player is dealt four cards, and four cards are dealt faceup in between the players. The rest of the cards are set aside as a Draw pile.

HOW TO PLAY:

Gameplay is trimmed down a bit for this two-player version. The two players simply take turns swapping cards from their hand with the four in the middle, hoping to get four of a kind. If no swaps are desired at any point, the four cards in the middle can be "trashed" and removed from the game, with four new cards being taken from the Draw pile. The first player to get four of a kind wins that round.

VARIATIONS:

The only variations to this game are for when it is played in teams.

GIN RUMMY

This classic game is simple to play but difficult to master, meaning it is ripe for repeat play between two players.

OBJECTIVE OF THE GAME: Build a hand of cards that maximizes the point value of matched cards while minimizing unmatched cards

MATERIALS: One standard deck of cards with the Jokers removed

HOW TO DEAL:

Each player is dealt 10 cards, and then one final card is played faceup to start the Discard pile. The rest of the deck is left as the Stock pile.

HOW TO PLAY:

In this game, cards rank low to high, with the Ace being low at 1 point value, all other face cards being worth 10 points each, and the numerical cards each being worth their respective number in points. You want to build sets and runs of cards in your hand, sets being three or four of a kind and runs being sequential value cards of the same suit.

Play consists of each player alternatively drawing and discarding cards each turn. Each player must draw one card and discard one card each turn. Cards can be drawn from either the Stock or the Discard pile. You cannot discard a card you just drew from the Discard pile. Discarded cards must be placed faceup on the Discard pile.

A player can end the round entirely (called "knocking") after drawing a card and then discarding a card facedown on the Discard pile. They then show their hand and what sets and/or runs they have. Any unmatched cards (called "deadwood") must be collectively worth 10 points or less. Knocking with no deadwood is called "going gin," which give you a bonus. You can knock at any time as long as you meet the requirement for your deadwood. You also aren't forced to knock at any time. The end will force an ending, though, once there are two cards left in the Stock pile.

When it comes to scoring at the end of a round, the difference between the unmatched cards is compared first. If the knocker's total is lower than the other player's, the knocker gets the difference in points. If the knocker's total is higher than the other player's, the other player scores the difference instead, plus an additional 10 points. If a player goes gin, then they score 20 more bonus points.

continued

Typically, the goal is 100 points, which can be played toward in multiple rounds. You can also just play to a best of three or five based on who scores more points each round.

VARIATIONS:

There are many variants to this game that you can search for online, the most popular being Oklahoma Gin.

LEVEL OF DIFFICULTY: HARD

LENGTH OF PLAY: 10 TO 20 MINUTES

ALTERNATIVE NAMES: NONE

CRIBBAGE

With roots going back to England in the 17th century to a game called Noddy, Cribbage enjoys continued popularity.

OBJECTIVE OF THE GAME: Be the first player to score a set number of points by combining various cards together

MATERIALS: One standard deck of cards with the Jokers removed

continued

HOW TO DEAL:

Players cut the deck to determine who deals. The player who chooses the lower card deals. Each player is dealt six cards, and they each choose which two cards from these to discard facedown to form the "crib" or the Discard pile. The deck is then cut by the non-dealer and then the top card of the lower half of the deck is placed faceup on the reunited deck.

HOW TO PLAY:

Play begins with the non-dealer playing a card from their hand, then the dealer alternatively does the same, with the goal of getting the value of the cards up to but not exceeding 31. Each numerical card is worth its number, the face cards are all worth 10, and Aces are worth 1. The running total is announced by each player as they play a card. If a player cannot play a card without exceeding 31, then they state "Go" to the other player, who can then reset the count and play out the rest of their hand to finish that cycle. Points can be scored in this phase as follows:

- If a player causes the count to hit exactly 15, they score 2 points.

- If a player completes a pair, they score 2 points.

- If a player completes three different pairs, they score 6 points.

- If a player completes four different pairs, they score 12 points.

- If a player completes a run of three or more consecutive value cards being played (not needing to be in value order; for example, if they put down a 6, you put down an 8, and then they put down a 7), they score the number of cards in the run (in this case, 3).

- Whenever "Go" is called, the last player to play a card scores 1 point if the running total is less than 31, or 2 points if the total is exactly 31.

When each player has finished, then the game progresses to the "show."

Starting with the non-dealer, each player displays their hand and scores it according to the point values outlined on page 96. If the Start Card was a Jack, the dealer gets two points. The crib is also scored in favor of the dealer. Whoever has the most points after this wins the round and is granted one additional point. Once the scores are tallied, the dealer role alternates to the other player and another round commences after shuffling all the cards back into the deck.

Typically, games are played to either 61 or 121 total points with several rounds. Scoring is often tracked on a Cribbage Board rather than on paper. You can also play to a best out of three or five.

VARIATIONS:
There are no known variations of this game.

LEVEL OF DIFFICULTY: HARD

LENGTH OF PLAY: 10 TO 20 MINUTES

ALTERNATIVE NAMES: NONE

HAND AND FOOT

A popular spin on Canasta, this game builds on the same rule base and can give players who enjoy Canasta a unique play experience.

OBJECTIVE OF THE GAME: Get as many points as you can from melding cards of the same rank

MATERIALS: Up to five standard decks of cards with the Jokers included (the number of decks depends on how long you want to play)

HOW TO DEAL:

Deal each player two sets of 11 cards. One set is the Hand, the other is the Foot. The rest of the cards form the Stock pile, from which the first card is drawn and placed faceup next to it to make the Discard pile. If the first card drawn is a red 3 or wild card (as in Canasta, Jokers and 2s are wild in this game), put it at the bottom of the Stock pile and draw another card.

HOW TO PLAY:

Players start the game using the Hand set of 11 cards. The Foot set of cards stays facedown in front of them.

Each player's turn begins by drawing two cards from the Stock pile. The top card from the Discard pile can be drawn instead if it is being used for a meld. Some rules state that if a card is being taken from the Discard pile, the entire pile (or up to seven cards) must be taken by that player so you can use one of these variations if you like.

After they draw, then players can make melds. Melds must be made up of at least three cards and can be composed of up to seven cards total. Melds also cannot have more wild cards than natural cards.

The player's turn ends by discarding one card. A black 3 being discarded blocks the Discard pile being used for melds. Black 3s cannot be melded.

Scoring is based on the value of the cards, how many are in each meld, and if any completed seven-card melds are "clean" or "dirty" (clean means no wild cards, dirty has wild cards). Here is a breakdown:

- Jokers = 50 points each
- Aces/2s = 20 points each
- Kings to 8s = 10 points each
- 7s to 4s = 5 points each
- Red 3s = 100 points each

continued

- Clean melds = 500 bonus points each

- Dirty melds = 300 bonus points each

With only two players and multiple decks of cards, it's best to make each round end when the first player hits a certain point threshold with their melds. Then, if you want to keep playing, you can reset and start again to determine who wins the best of three or five rounds.

VARIATIONS:

There are no known variations of this game.

CHAPTER 6

TRICK-TAKING GAMES

EUCHRE

Another historic game with roots and predecessors dating back to 18th century Europe, Euchre has a simple premise that is accessible to any player.

OBJECTIVE OF THE GAME: Score points by having the highest ranked card and get to 10 points before your opponent

MATERIALS: One standard deck of cards with the 2s through 8s and Jokers removed, leaving 24 cards

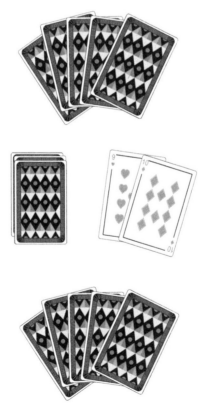

HOW TO DEAL:

When playing with two players, the dealer is chosen by a coin toss. The dealer gives each player eight cards. Each player must have five cards in their hand before the game begins, so three cards must be discarded into the shuffled deck of remaining cards, which are placed in the middle of the table facedown as the Draw pile.

HOW TO PLAY:

Play begins with the non-dealer turning over the card from the top of the Draw pile to determine the trump suit. The non-dealer player can accept the suit of this card as the trump suit or have the other player choose a different suit. If the suit of the flipped card is chosen, then the dealer swaps one of the cards in their hand with the flipped card. If the suit is not chosen, then the card remains.

Aces are high in Euchre, and the Jack of the trump suit is the highest ranked card. Additionally, the Jack of the same-color off suit joins the trump suit, ranking just below the Jack of the trump suit (second-highest).

The non-dealer plays first after the trump suit is determined. The non-dealer places a card at the center of the table and then the other player tries to place a card of higher rank. Whichever player put down the higher rank card takes the cards (otherwise known as a trick). The winner of that trick goes first in the next round.

When playing with two players, once both players empty their hands, they can draw five new cards to get the game to the winning total of 10 points. Each trick is worth 1 point.

VARIATIONS:

You can play this game with more players, more cards in each hand, or other specialty rules. Do an online search for other versions such as British Euchre or Buck Euchre.

LEVEL OF DIFFICULTY: EASY

LENGTH OF PLAY: 10 TO 15 MINUTES

ALTERNATIVE NAMES: NONE

SIXTY-SIX

Similar to Euchre, this game has a unique scoring system and usually will run for slightly longer.

OBJECTIVE OF THE GAME: Take the most tricks to get to 66 points

MATERIALS: One standard deck of cards with the 2s, 3s, 4s, 5s, 6s, 7s, 8s, and Jokers removed, leaving 24 cards

HOW TO DEAL:

After using a coin toss to determine the dealer, the dealer gives each player six cards. The top card from the remaining cards determines the trump suit. That pile is the Stock to draw from for the rest of the game. The card pulled to determine the trump suit is placed back into the middle of the Stock pile.

HOW TO PLAY:

The non-dealer starts play by placing one of the cards from their hand into the middle of the table. The other player must try to outrank this card. Rankings have Aces high and the trump suit winning over any tied ranks. Winning this play is called a "trick." The winner of the trick draws a card first from the Stock pile and plays a card first the next turn.

After all the cards have been played, players tally up the scores from their tricks as follows:

- Each Ace = 11 points
- Each 10 = 10 points
- Each King = 4 points
- Each Queen = 3 points
- Each Jack = 2 points

- Last trick = 10 points
- King and Queen of trump suit = 20 points
- King and Queen of trump suit won in a single trick = 20 points

Whichever player wins 66 points (or is closest to it) wins the round. Players can continue to play to see who wins the best of five or seven rounds.

VARIATIONS:

There are no known variations of this game.

LEVEL OF DIFFICULTY: MEDIUM

LENGTH OF PLAY: 5 TO 10 MINUTES

ALTERNATIVE NAMES: SIPA, AGRAM, JEU DE CARTE

SPAR

This trick-taking card game that originated in Ghana does not have trumps, distinguishing it from most of its peers.

OBJECTIVE OF THE GAME: Win the last trick in each round

MATERIALS: One standard deck of cards with the 2s, 3s, 4s, 5s, Jokers, and the Ace of Spades removed, leaving 35 cards.

HOW TO DEAL:

Flip a coin to determine the dealer, who then gives each player five cards. The remaining cards are put facedown in between the players.

HOW TO PLAY:

The non-dealer starts play by placing faceup the first card from their hand in between the two players. It can be any card the player chooses from their hand. The other player seeks to put down a card of higher rank to win the trick. Aces are high in this game. The cards are not gathered after each trick, but the winner of each trick places their card first.

The simplest way to play this game is to determine the winner of each round of five tricks by whoever wins the fifth and final trick, then keep playing to see who wins the best of five or seven rounds. The skill here is trying to figure out what is the best card to keep in your hand until the end since the other player is trying to do the same.

VARIATIONS:

The other alternative titles of this game have variant rules, but the crux of much of the changes to play are the number of cards in each player's hand, the number of cards in the deck, and/or adding points in to determine the overall winner.

PINOCHLE

A unique trick-taking game, Pinochle combines classic elements of this game type with the melding found in matching games.

OBJECTIVE OF THE GAME: Score as many points as you can through winning cards and making melds from those cards

MATERIALS: Two standard decks of cards with the 2s, 3s, 4s, 5s, 6s, 7s, 8s, and Jokers removed, leaving 48 cards total

HOW TO DEAL:

Flip a coin to determine the dealer. Each player is dealt 12 cards from the shuffled deck. The remaining cards are placed facedown in between the two players, with the top card from this Stock pile turned over at the start of the game to determine the trump suit. This card remains visible throughout play.

HOW TO PLAY:

The ranking in Pinochle is a bit different from other games, with Aces being the highest, followed by 10s, Kings, Queens, Jacks, and 9s (9s are the lowest rank).

Gameplay starts with the non-dealer playing their first card from their hand. Players are not required to follow suit when playing cards. The player with the higher rank card wins the trick and takes the two cards, putting them aside facedown. They also draw the first card from the Stock pile and play the next card. This cycle continues until the Stock pile is depleted.

While this cycle of turns goes on, each player can create melds of the cards in their hand. These melds score the player points on the following scale:

- Sequence in the trump suit (in order of Ace, King, Queen, Jack, 10) = 150 points

- Marriage (King and Queen of trump suit) = 40 points

- Marriage (King and Queen of non-trump suit) = 20 points

- 4 Aces = 100 points

- 4 Kings = 80 points

- 4 Queens = 60 points

- 4 Jacks = 40 points

- Pinochle (Queen of Spades and Jack of Diamonds) = 40 points

Points are tallied as the melds are made. Melded cards can still be played each turn.

continued

Once the Stock gets down to its last card plus the trump suit–indicating card, the winner of the preceding trick can choose which card to draw. After this, all melded cards return to the respective player's hands, and the turns continue until all the cards are played into the players' trick piles. Melding is not allowed during this phase of the game. The winner of the last trick gets 10 extra points.

The final score tally includes accounting for the cards in each player's trick pile:

- Aces = 11 points
- 10s = 10 points
- Kings = 4 points
- Queens = 3 points
- Jacks = 2 points
- 9s = 0 points

Winning the last trick of a round also scores 10 additional points.

The winner of the entire game is the first person to get 1200 total points.

VARIATIONS:
There are some simple variants to this game where you play to different point totals or where you score cards slightly differently so that everything stays even versus having odd numbered scores.

LEVEL OF DIFFICULTY: HARD

LENGTH OF PLAY: 10 TO 20 MINUTES

ALTERNATIVE NAME: NORWEGIAN WHIST

WHIST

This unique trick-taking game has Scandinavian roots and involves playing two cards at once.

OBJECTIVE OF THE GAME: Win as many tricks as you can (or avoid them), depending on whether the game is played "high" or "low."

MATERIALS: One standard deck of cards with the Jokers removed

continued

HOW TO DEAL:

Flip a coin to determine the dealer. The dealer alternates giving cards to each player, with each player given 8 cards facedown in a rectangle consisting of 2 rows with 4 cards each. Then, 8 cards are put faceup on top of each of those cards. Finally, 10 cards are given to each player's hand.

HOW TO PLAY:

The non-dealer states first whether the round is high or low, which determines whether the players will be aiming to win as many or as few tricks as possible. The dealer can respond to this statement as well most of the time. For example, if the non-dealer says high, and the dealer does not respond, and it is a high game. If the non-dealer says low, the dealer can also say low, and then it is a low game. If the non-dealer says low and then the dealer says high, then it is a high game.

If it is a low game, the non-dealer plays first. If it is a high game, then the player who did not say high plays first. Any card from the player's hand or from the faceup cards in front of them can be played. The first card (called the "lead card" and the player who put it down is called the "leader") played for each turn sets the suit for the other cards played. The next player must play a card if it follows the suit and is in their hand or faceup in front of them. If a faceup card is played, then the card beneath it is immediately turned faceup. Players alternate each playing two cards each turn for four cards total between them. The player with the highest rank card of the lead suit wins the trick. There are no set trump suits in this game and Aces are high. The player who wins the trick leads the next turn.

Once all the cards in each player's hand and in front of them are gone, scoring is tallied up according to whether it was a high or low game:

In a high game, whoever bid high at the beginning gets one point for every trick they won over 6, so if they won 8 tricks in the round, they would get 2 points. If this player does not win more than 6 tricks, then the other player gets 2 points for each trick above 6.

In a low game, the player with the least number of tricks scores a point for each trick less than 7 they won. For example, if the final number of tricks between players was 9 to 4, then the player with 4 tricks would get 3 points.

The winner at the very end is whoever gets to 13 total points or higher.

VARIATIONS:
There are no known variations of this game.

LEVEL OF DIFFICULTY: HARD

LENGTH OF PLAY: 10 TO 20 MINUTES

ALTERNATIVE NAME: CALL BRIDGE

SPADES

Usually played with four players, this version of the game only differs in the way the cards are initially dealt.

OBJECTIVE OF THE GAME: Predict how many tricks you'll win to score more points than your opponent

MATERIALS: One standard deck of cards with the Jokers removed

HOW TO DEAL:

From a facedown shuffled deck, each player takes turns drawing two cards, one at a time. They either choose to keep the first card and then discard the other or vice versa. The goal here is to get the highest rank cards you can in your hand to start the game. Both players alternatively do this until they each have 13 cards in their hand. All the remaining cards not in a player's hand are shuffled back together.

HOW TO PLAY:

Before actual play begins, each player must make a prediction, called a "bid," where they say how many tricks they expect to win this round. It must be at least one. Players get more points the more tricks they make and the closer they get to their bid. It is better to go over than under, since if you don't hit your bids, then you get no points, but if you go over, then you get one point for each trick you win over your bids. For example, if you make a bid of 6 tricks, but win 7 tricks, you'd end the round scoring 10 points for each of the 6 tricks, and then one point for the extra trick for a total of 61 points. But if you had made a bid of 8 tricks, you'd end the round with zero points.

Gameplay follows your standard trick-taking formula of players taking turns trying to play the higher rank card to win the trick. Whoever plays the first card forces the other player to follow the suit of the card they played if the other player has a card to play of that suit. If a player cannot follow suit, they can play any card in their hand. Spades trump all other suited cards no matter the rank of the spade suit card. Also, Aces are high in this game and cards are not drawn during each round. If a player wins the trick, they take the whole pile of cards beneath. Play continues until each player depletes their hand.

Players continue in rounds until someone earns 500 total points and wins the game.

VARIATIONS:

Some possible variants for Spades include deducting points if you go over your number of bids, allowing for "nil bids" where the player predicts winning no tricks, and including Jokers as the ultimate trump card.

CHAPTER 7

VYING GAMES

BINGO

Much like the classic game of the same name, this game is a luck-based activity that can help pass the time.

OBJECTIVE OF THE GAME: Be the first player to play down the cards in your hand

MATERIALS: Two standard decks of cards with the Jokers removed

HOW TO DEAL:

Each player is dealt five cards faceup from one of the shuffled decks. The other deck is for calling the cards for the other players to match.

HOW TO PLAY:

Although this game is meant to be played with more than two people, you can make Bingo work for two players by simply have one of the players draw a card from the other deck and let both players see what was drawn.

As a player has a match for a card (of rank and suit) in their hand, they turn that card facedown. Once all their cards are facedown, they win the round. You can extend play by adding more cards to each player's hand, or play to see who wins the best of five or seven rounds.

VARIATIONS:

There are no known variations of this game.

GOLF

Golf is essentially a card game version of the sport of the same name, where the goal there is also to get the lowest score possible.

OBJECTIVE OF THE GAME: Earn the fewest number of points over the course of nine deals

MATERIALS: One standard deck of cards with the Jokers removed

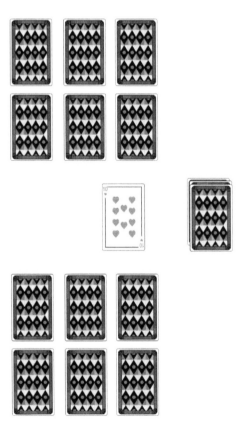

HOW TO DEAL:

Deal six facedown cards to each player in two rows of three. The rest of the deck forms the Stock pile, and the top card is turned over to create the Discard pile next to it.

HOW TO PLAY:

Play begins with the first player drawing a card from the Stock or Discard pile.

They can decide to swap this card with one in front of them or to discard this card. An important thing to note: If a card is drawn from the Discard pile, it must be played and not just returned to the Discard pile. If the player doesn't swap in the drawn card from the Stock pile, they can flip over one of the cards in front of them or do nothing their turn. Players should always have six cards in front of them.

The next player repeats this maneuver and play continues until all six cards in front of one of the players are faceup. The other player can get one more turn after this and then the round is over.

Each player's hand is then scored as follows:

- Each Ace = add 1 point
- Each 2 = minus 2 points
- Each numeric card from 3 to 10 = add face value in points

- Each Jack or Queen = add 10 points
- A pair of equal cards = 0 points

A full game is typically nine hands (or "holes") and the player with the lowest cumulative score is the winner. You can also play up to 19 hands if you like.

VARIATIONS:

There are no known variations of this game.

GUTS

Simple enough to play with younger children, this is a game of luck and your ability to bluff others in or out of the game.

OBJECTIVE OF THE GAME: Have the highest-ranking pair of cards to win the pot

MATERIALS: One standard deck of cards with the Jokers removed; betting chips

HOW TO DEAL:

Each player is given the same amount of chips and then is dealt two cards facedown from a shuffled deck. Players must each put one chip into the pot and can look at their own cards when the game begins.

HOW TO PLAY:

After viewing their cards, each player determines if they are in or out of the round. They must guess if their pair (if they have one) is better than the other player's pair (if they have one). Basic poker rules apply in terms of the value of a pair, where a pair of 10s would beat a pair of 5s. A pair of Aces is the best hand a player can get.

When playing with two players (this game can be played with up to 10 players), it is most likely that both players will always stay in since the other player automatically wins the pot if they don't. If there is a tie in the value of the pairs, the pot is split and then replenished with one chip from each player before the next round.

VARIATIONS:

There are many different ways to play this game, such as dealing more cards to each player, not allowing players to look at their cards before betting, and playing with a "dummy" hand for a nonexistent player who must be beaten.

BLACKJACK

A classic casino game, Blackjack can easily be played with two players and perfectly blends luck and skill. The rules we'll cover here are simplified to remove the premise of betting.

OBJECTIVE OF THE GAME: Build your hand to get as close in value to 21 without going over

MATERIALS: One standard deck of cards with the Jokers removed

HOW TO DEAL:

To start, flip a coin to determine who will be the dealer. Then, the dealer will lay down one card faceup and one card facedown for themselves and then two cards faceup to the player.

HOW TO PLAY:

The player is essentially competing with the dealer when there are just two players. The first thing that must be determined is whether either player got a natural 21, since this automatically wins the hand. Card values are fairly simple: Aces can be either 1 or 11 depending on what the player wants, numeric cards are worth their respective numeral, and face cards are all worth 10. The way to get a natural 21 is if a player gets a face card or a 10 and an Ace. The dealer can check their facedown card if the faceup card is a face card, an Ace, or a 10. If both the player and the dealer get natural 21s, then the hand is deemed a draw and everything is reset.

Play starts with the non-dealer choosing to "hit" to get another card or "stand" to not get another card. This determination is made depending on how close the player's cards are to 21. If the total value of the player's cards goes over 21, then they have gone "bust" and automatically lose this hand.

Once the non-dealer is done, then the dealer turns over their facedown card. If the total value of their cards is 16 or under, they must hit. If the total value is 17 or above, they stay.

Then, compare total card values between the two players' hands and whoever is closest to 21 without going over is the winner of the round. The roles then can be swapped for each subsequent round. Typically, players would continue play to see who wins the best of five or seven rounds.

VARIATIONS:

There are no known variations of this game.

LEVEL OF DIFFICULTY: HARD

LENGTH OF PLAY: 5 TO 10 MINUTES

ALTERNATIVE NAMES: NONE

FIVE-CARD STUD POKER

Primarily focused on betting and winning money, this card game has roots back to the 1860s in America and remains popular today in casinos. We'll focus on the core rules here and let players determine how and if they want to bet money while they play. If players wish, they can use chips to determine how much they want to risk each time a card is dealt for each player, which will add the elements of skill and bluffing.

OBJECTIVE OF THE GAME: Be the player with the best five-card hand

MATERIALS: One standard deck of cards with the Jokers removed; betting chips (optional)

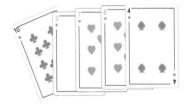

HOW TO DEAL:

Each player is dealt one card facedown and one card faceup. Then, they are dealt one card faceup at a time until each player has five cards faceup in front of them in addition to the one facedown card (often referred to as the "hole" card).

HOW TO PLAY:

When each player has the five cards laid out in front of them, they can then turn over their facedown card and determine the best five-card hand they can make with the six cards available to them. The ranking of hands falls in line with classic poker rules. For a refresher, here they are in order from low to high:

- Pair = two cards of equal rank

- Two pairs = two sets of two cards of equal rank

- Three of a kind = three cards of equal rank

- Straight = five cards in sequence of any suit

- Flush = five cards of the same suit

- Full house = three cards of equal rank with two cards of another equal rank

- Four of a kind = four cards of equal rank

- Straight flush = five cards of the same suit in sequence

- Royal flush = straight flush from 10 to Ace

When determining who has a better pair, for example, a pair of 10s would beat a pair of 5s. This applies to all the hands outlined here. The player with the higher-ranking hand wins the round. Rounds can be played as many times as desired.

VARIATIONS:

There are several variants to this game. To learn more, do an online search for Lowball, California Stud, or Seven-Card Stud.

LEVEL OF DIFFICULTY: HARD

LENGTH OF PLAY: 5 TO 10 MINUTES

ALTERNATIVE NAMES: NONE

TEXAS HOLD 'EM

Currently the most popular version of poker, this game is fun to watch because of the emphasis on bluffing and prediction. It can be played without betting real money by using chips instead.

OBJECTIVE OF THE GAME: Build the best five-card hand possible using your cards plus the community cards

MATERIALS: One standard deck of cards with Jokers removed; betting chips

HOW TO DEAL:

To start, each player is dealt two cards facedown (known as "hole cards"). Five community cards will be dealt throughout the hand. Betting chips should be split between players.

HOW TO PLAY:

In poker, players try to create sets of cards from their hand and the community cards. The sets they can make, ranked from lowest value to highest, is as follows:

- Pair = two cards of equal rank

- Two pairs = two sets of two cards of equal rank

- Three of a kind = three cards of equal rank

- Straight = five cards in sequence of any suit

- Flush = five cards of the same suit

- Full house = three cards of equal rank with two cards of another equal rank

- Four of a kind = four cards of equal rank

- Straight flush = five cards of the same suit in sequence

- Royal flush = straight flush from 10 to Ace

Based on the sets that players think they can make, they bet as many chips as they want (or money, if desired). Players can choose to either "check" to pass to the other player, "open" a bet if none has been placed yet, "call" to match a bet that has been played, or "raise" the bet to force the other player to call their bet amount. This is where the strategy of the game comes in; you're applying pressure to the other player to gauge their confidence in their own hand. Players will have four different opportunities to make or change their bets.

continued

Once the hands have been dealt, players look at their hands and make their first bets. Then, three community cards are dealt faceup on the table, called "the flop." Players make their bets again, trying to consider what cards could possibly still be in play given what cards are in their hands and what has already been dealt in the flop.

Then, another card is dealt into the center, the "turn," and players again make bets. The fifth card, the "river," is then dealt into the center, and players make their final bets.

Once final bets have been made, the players reveal their hands to each other. The person with the highest-ranking set combined with the community cards wins the betted chips. Players can continue for as many rounds as they'd like.

VARIATIONS:
There are many fun versions of this game. Do an online search for Omaha Hold 'Em, Double Texas Hold 'Em, or Greek Hold 'Em.

INDEX

ABOUT THE AUTHOR

 **DUSTIN RAMSDELL** is a blogger, podcaster, and proud geek who has been creating content consistently for the past eight years. He works professionally in higher education technology, helping to support students' successes every day. Dustin loves games of all kinds and enjoys sharing in the fun with others. He relaxes by watching the latest superhero movie, reading about current events, taking long walks, and drinking good coffee. You might also find him at the local craft beer brewery. Dustin lives in Delaware with his wife, Jenn; his daughter, Eleanor; and his dog, Chelsea.